D1737706

FIRST TOUCH SOCCER

F.C. BARCELONA

BY
MARK STEWART

NORWOOD HOUSE PRESS
Chicago, Illinois

NORWOOD HOUSE PRESS

P.O. Box 316598 • Chicago, Illinois 60631
For more information about Norwood House Press please visit our website at
www.norwoodhousepress.com or call 866-565-2900.

Photography and Collectibles:
The trading cards and other memorabilia assembled in the background for this book's cover and interior pages
are all part of the author's collection and are reproduced for educational and artistic purposes.

All photos courtesy of Associated Press except the following individual photos and artifacts (page numbers):
Author's Collection (6, 10 both, 11 middle), LFP Trading Cards (11 top & bottom, 16),
Juego del 5 (23).

Cover image: Emilio Morenatti/Associated Press

Designer: Ron Jaffe
Series Editor: Mike Kennedy
Content Consultants: Michael Jacobsen and Jonathan Wentworth-Ping
Project Management: Black Book Partners, LLC
Editorial Production: Lisa Walsh

LIBRARY OF CONGRESS CATALOGING-IN-PUBLICATION DATA
Names: Stewart, Mark, 1960 July 7- author.
Title: F.C. Barcelona / By Mark Stewart.
Other titles: Futbol Club Barcelona
Description: Chicago, Illinois : Norwood House Press, 2017. | Series: First
    Touch Soccer | Includes bibliographical references and index. | Audience:
    Age 5-8. | Audience: K to Grade 3.
Identifiers: LCCN 2016058196 (print) | LCCN 2017005788 (ebook) | ISBN
    9781599538594 (library edition : alk. paper) | ISBN 9781684040780 (eBook)
Subjects: LCSH: Futbol Club Barcelona--History--Juvenile literature.
Classification: LCC GV943.6.B3 S74 2017 (print) | LCC GV943.6.B3 (ebook) |
    DDC 796.334/64094672--dc23
LC record available at https://lccn.loc.gov/2016058196

302N--072017
Manufactured in the United States of America in North Mankato, Minnesota.

CONTENTS

Words in **bold type** are defined on page 24.

In soccer, star players often go by a one-word nickname. In this book, we use the nickname followed by the player's (*full name*).

Lionel Messi gives his teammate Neymar (*Neymar da Silva Santos Junior*) some love after scoring a goal in a 2016 match.

MEET F.C. BARCELONA

Is a soccer team truly part of its hometown? In Barcelona it is. The city is in the Catalonia region of Spain, which has its own language and culture. Its team is called Futbol Club Barcelona. When people say "futbol" in Spain they are talking about soccer, not American football.

Barcelona fans call their club "Barca" for short. On **match** days, you can hear their chants of *Barca! Barca! Barca!* throughout the city.

TIME MACHINE

In the fall of 1899, a young athlete named Hans Gamper placed an ad in a Barcelona newspaper. It said he was forming a soccer club in the city and invited people to play. Barcelona soon became one of the best teams in Spain.

During the 1950s, Barcelona started to add foreign players to the team. They helped the club become a world power. Their great stars include **Laszlo Kubala**, Johan Cruyff, Hristo Stoichkov, and Luis Figo.

KUBALA
Club de Futbol Barcelona
Campeón de España 1950 51

Hristo Stoichkov dribbles past a defender in a 1997 match. Stoichkov was a star in Bulgaria before joining Barcelona.

Sometimes in Camp Nou, the fans are as much a part of the show as the players!

BEST SEAT IN THE HOUSE

Barcelona plays in a stadium called Camp Nou. Camp Nou is Calatan for New Field. It was "new" when it opened in 1957. It will be new again in 2021, when it is enlarged. It holds more than 99,000 fans now. That makes Camp Nou the largest stadium in Europe.

COLLECTOR'S CORNER

These collectibles show some of the best Barcelona players ever.

SUAREZ LUIS

LUIS SUAREZ

Midfielder

1955–1961

Suarez was a graceful passer with a powerful shot. He was the first Spanish player to be named the top player in Europe.

XAVIER HERNANDEZ

Midfielder

1998–2015

No one played more games for Barcelona than "Xavi." He was *World Soccer* magazine's Player of the Year in 2010.

F.C. Barcelona

RONALDINHO

Midfielder/Forward

2003–2008

Ronaldinho (*Ronaldo de Assis Moreira*) was always on the attack. He made passes and shots no one had ever seen before.

ANDRES INIESTA

Midfielder

First Year with Club: 2002

Iniesta brought fans to their feet with his amazing **ball control**. His skills made all of his teammates better.

070   Iniesta

LIONEL MESSI

Forward

First Year with Club: 2004

Messi used his small size and quick moves to become the best player in the world. He scored more than 300 goals for Barcelona.

WORTHY OPPONENTS

Barcelona and Real Madrid are the two strongest teams in the Spanish League. The two cities are fierce rivals and so are their fans. Matches between the two clubs are nicknamed El Clasico, which is Spanish for The Classic. Long ago, only championship matches had this name. Now every game between the two clubs does.

Sergio Busquets tries to stop Mariano Diaz from scoring during a 2016 match. The matches between Barcelona and Real Madrid can get very physical.

CLUB WAYS

Barcelona fans are known for their loud chants. When 100,000 people yell at the same time, you can feel it in your bones. Their favorite chant is taken from a church song about the city. It ends with the words "We've got the name that everyone knows … *Barca! Barca! Baaaaarca!*"

Barca fans form a sea of red, yellow, and blue at an away game in Germany.

Barcelona brings together players from many countries. These are some of the best:

1. **Michael Laudrup** • Frederiksberg, Denmark
2. **Thierry Henry** • Les Ulis, France
3. **Luis Figo** • Almada, Portugal ➜
4. **Sandor Kocsis** • Budapest, Hungary
5. **Julio Cesar Benitez** • Montevideo, Uruguay
6. **Diego Maradona** • Buenos Aires, Argentina
7. **Samuel Eto'o** • Douala, Cameroon
8. **Paulina Alcantara** • Iloilo City, Philippines

NORTH

WEST EAST

SOUTH

MAP OF EUROPE

F.C. Barcelona's home stadium is in Barcelona, Spain.

WORLD MAP

Sergio Busquets wears the club's home kit, which has a crest on the chest and sleeve.

KIT AND CREST

Barcelona players wear blue and red shirts with blue shorts for home games. The away **kit** is mostly black. The uniform changes a little bit from year to year. The club's crest was designed more than 100 years ago. It is a shield with a cross, the flag of Catalonia, and the team colors.

WE WON!

Most soccer fans believe that Barcelona's team in 2008–09 was its best ever. That season, the club won the Spanish League and the Copa del Rey, which is Spanish for King's Cup. They went on to win the Champions League. The Champions League is the toughest tournament in Europe. Barcelona defeated Manchester United in the final, 2–0. Samuel Eto'o and Lionel Messi scored for Barca.

Lionel Messi and Andres Iniesta hold up the Champions League trophy after defeating Manchester United in 2009.

FOR THE RECORD

Barcelona has won more than
60 major championships!

Copa del Rey

28 (From 1910 to 2014)

Super Cup

1992, 1997, 2009, 2011 & 2015

European Cup/Champions League

1991–92
2005–06
2008–09
2010–11
2014–15

Spanish League

24 championships
(from 1928–29 to 2015–16)

Club World Cup

2008–09
2010–11
2012–13

Cup Winners' Cup

1978–79
1981–82
1988–89
1996–97

These stars won major awards while playing for Barcelona:

1960	Luis Suarez • European Footballer of the Year
1973	Johan Cruyff • European Footballer of the Year
1974	Johan Cruyff • European Footballer of the Year
1994	Hristo Stoichkov • European Footballer of the Year
1994	Romario (*Romario de Souza Faria*) World Player of the Year
1996	Ronaldo (*Ronaldo Luis Nazario de Lima*) World Player of the Year
1999	Rivaldo (*Rivaldo Vitor Borba Ferreira*) European Footballer of the Year
1999	**Rivaldo** • World Player of the Year
2004	Ronaldinho • World Player of the Year
2005	Ronaldinho • European Footballer of the Year
2005	Ronaldinho • World Player of the Year
2009	Lionel Messi • European Footballer of the Year
2010	Lionel Messi • World Footballer of the Year
2011	Lionel Messi • World Footballer of the Year
2012	Lionel Messi • World Footballer of the Year
2015	Lionel Messi • World Footballer of the Year

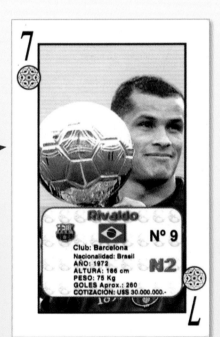

Soccer Words

Index

Ball Control
The ability to shoot, pass, and change direction quickly without losing the ball to a defender.

Kit
The official league equipment of soccer players, including a club's uniform.

Match
Another word for game. Soccer matches are 90 minutes long. Each half is 45 minutes, with a 15-minute break in between.

Photos are on **BOLD** numbered pages.

About the Author

Mark Stewart has been writing about world soccer since the 1990s, including *Soccer: A History of the World's Most Popular Game.* In 2005, he co-authored Major League Soccer's 10-year anniversary book.

About F.C. Barcelona

Learn more at these websites:
www.fcbarcelona.com/en
www.fifa.com
www.teamspiritextras.com